THE CELTIC CHOIR

An Acoustic Praise Choral Collection

BY
JOSEPH M. MARTIN
CONSORT ORCHESTRATION BY STAN PETHEL

ISBN 978-1-4803-6105-8

EXCLUSIVELY DISTRIBUTED BY

HAL•LEONARD®
CORPORATION

7777 W. BLUEMOUND RD. P.O. BOX 13819 MILWAUKEE, WI 53213

Visit Shawnee Press Online at
www.shawneepress.com

FOREWORD

The folk music of the British Isles has inspired the imagination of musicians everywhere for centuries. In recent years, Celtic-styled music has emerged as one of the most influential forces in contemporary popular music. Modern sacred music has also been influenced by this great treasury of music and poetry. Many new hymns and anthems are based on Celtic themes and musical gestures. Filled with rich style and purpose, these timeless tunes have the power to animate our sanctuaries with jubilant praise or to touch our hearts with quiet comfort and hope.

In this compilation, you will find Celtic-styled choral pieces ideal for use during Lent, Holy Week and Eastertide. *The Celtic Choir* is part of our "Acoustic Praise" series of publications. In it, each selection has the option for you to add a small consort of instruments to your presentation to create an authentic, folk style. It is our prayer that you will find *The Celtic Choir* to be a helpful addition to your choral library.

Let the music begin!

JOSEPH M. MARTIN

written in celebration of the life of Jennifer McMahon

CELTIC PRAISE SONG

for S.A.T.B. voices, accompanied

Words by
JOSEPH M. MARTIN (BMI)
Quoting
"I Sing the Mighty Power of God"
by ISAAC WATTS (1674-1748)

Music by
JOSEPH M. MARTIN (BMI)
Incorporating Tune:
KINGSFOLD
Traditional English Melody

With joyous abandon (♩. = ca. 60)

lu - ia! Re-joice with glad mu - sic._____ Al-le - lu - ia! Give thanks to the_

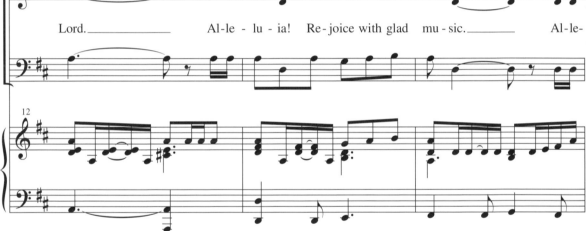

Lord._____ Al-le - lu - ia! Re-joice with glad mu - sic._____ Al-le-

lu - ia! Re-joice ev - er - more. Al-le - lu - ia! Re-joice with glad

Come, sing un - to the Lord a great song of thanks-giv - ing.

Serve with glad - ness for all of your days.

Come, bring un - to the Lord, and give thanks with your liv - ing.

O___ sing the might - y

pow'r of God that_ made the moun - tains rise; that___

* Tune: KINGSFOLD, traditional English melody
Words: Isaac Watts, 1674-1748

THE CELTIC CHOIR - SATB

spread the flow - ing seas a-broad, and built the loft - y skies. O sing the wis - dom that or - dained the sun to rule the day.

The__ moon shines full at His com-mand, and__

all the stars__ o - bey, and__ all the stars__ o - bey.

Al - le - lu - ia! Al - le - lu - ia! Give all glo - ry to

God! Come, sing un-to the Lord with a song of thanks-giv-ing. Serve with glad-ness for all of your days. Come, bring un-to the Lord, and give thanks with your liv-ing.

We are a peo - ple of praise.

We are a peo - ple of praise. Al - le - lu - ia!

We are a peo - ple of praise!

IN THE VALLEY FLOWS A RIVER

for S.A.T.B. voices, accompanied

Words by
DOUGLAS NOLAN (BMI)
and **PAMELA STEWART** (BMI)

Music by
DOUGLAS NOLAN (BMI)
Adapted by
JOSEPH M. MARTIN (BMI)

14

drink____ there will____ nev - er thirst for more.   In the

val - ley flows a riv - er, cool-ing stream   that has no

end._____   In its grace   we find for-give - ness, cleans-ing

THE CELTIC CHOIR - SATB

foun - tain for our sins.

From the moun - tain___ springs, it com - eth___ to the

des - ert, to the plains;___ bring - ing life to all it

16

touch - es, bring - ing peace where there is pain. In the

val - ley there is com - fort, where the peace - ful wa - ters

flow; and___ all who pause and pray___ there will___

find _____ rest for _____ their souls. _____ In the

val – ley flows a riv – er fed by heav – en's gen – tle

rain; and _____ all who stop and drink _____ there will _____

nev - er thirst a - gain; and__ all who stop and

drink__ there will__ nev - er thirst a - gain.

dedicated to the Glory of God and the observance of the 100th anniversary
of Grace United Church of Christ, Hanover, PA, July 9, 2006

THE MASTER HAS COME
(from "Footprints in the Sand")
for S.A.T.B. voices, accompanied

Tune: **ASH GROVE**
Welsh Folk Tune
Arranged by
JOSEPH M. MARTIN (BMI)

Words by
SARAH DOUDNEY (1841-1926)

22

band.

We love Him, we seek Him, we

long to be near Him, and rest in the light of His

beau - ti - ful land.

God's Ho - ly__ Spir - it shall com - fort__ the__ wea - ry. We

shall

fol - low__ the__ Sav - ior and can - not turn back. The__

Mas - ter__ has__ called us. Though doubt and__ temp - ta - tion may

Come,* come, come, come. May

com - pass___ our___ jour - ney, we cheer - ful - ly sing.___

cresc.

"Press___ on - ward, look___ up - ward." Through much trib - u -

la - tion, the chil - dren___ of___ Zi - on must fol - low their

King._____

mf

cresc. poco a poco

f

90

unis.

The   Mas - ter   has___ called___ us___ in

f unis.

f

92

life's_ ear - ly___ morn - ing,___ with   spir - its___ as___ fresh   as   the

spir - its   fresh___ as___ the___

Lyrics:

dew on the sod. We turn from the

world, with its smiles and its scorn - ing, to cast in our

cast our

lot with the peo - ple of God. The

28

commissioned by the Sanctuary Choir of Belmont Baptist Church, Charlottesville, Virginia,
to the glory of God and in honor of Gloria Johnson for 40 faithful years of service as organist

A CELTIC HOSANNA
(from "Canticle of the Cross")
for S.A.T.B. voices, accompanied

Words by
JOSEPH M. MARTIN

Based on tune: **ST. DENIO**
Traditional Welsh Tune
Arranged by
JOSEPH M. MARTIN (BMI)

Ho - san - na, ho - san - na, let voic - es now ring!

With palms raised in tri - umph and psalms raised in praise,

32

unis.

to Christ high ex - alt - ed, our

songs now___ we___ raise.

way; and shout to the na - tions: "the King has come____ to-

day."

The____

36

THE CELTIC CHOIR - SATB

san - na, ho - san - na, let the gates o - pen wide.

Ho - san - na, ho - san - na, in tri - umph He

rides.   Our

40

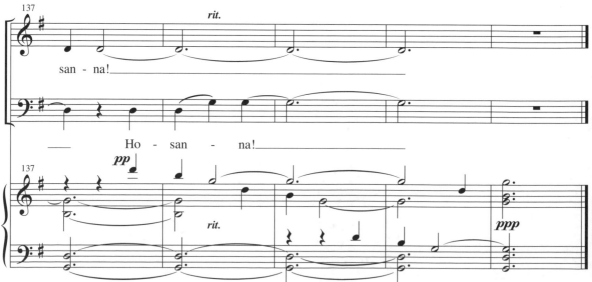

COME TO THE UPPER ROOM

(from "Canticle of the Cross")

for S.A.T.B. voices, accompanied

Words by
JOSEPH M. MARTIN

Traditional English Melody
Arranged by
JOSEPH M. MARTIN (BMI)

44

THE CELTIC CHOIR - SATB

46

THE CELTIC CHOIR - SATB

room.   There's a   place   of for-give - ness and mer - cy.

Come_ to the up - per room.___   Come,   all   who are wound - ed,

all who__ mourn, and Christ will give you peace._____

commissioned by the Springhill United Methodist Church Chancel Choir, Springhill, Louisiana,
in honor of Dr. Gene Wilson Kelsay, Minister of Music for 32 years

HERE IS LOVE

(from "Covenant of Grace")

for S.A.T.B. voices, accompanied

Words by
WILLIAM REES (1802-1883) *alt.*

Tune:
DYMA GARIAD
by ROBERT LOWRY (1826-1899)
Arranged by
JOSEPH M. MARTIN (BMI)

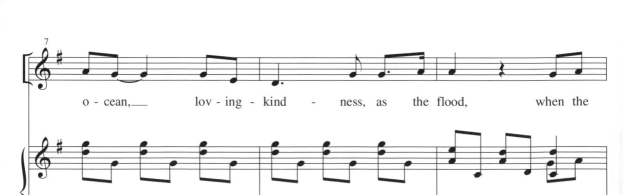

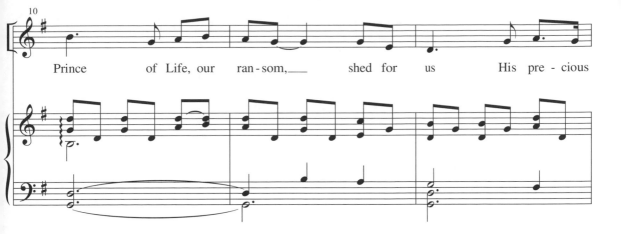

Prince of Life, our ran-som,___ shed for us His pre-cious

blood. Who His love will not re-mem-ber?___ Who can

TENOR

BASS

cease to sing His praise? He can nev - er be for-

52

peace___ and per-fect jus-tice___ kissed a guilt - y world in

love.___ Grace and love, like might-y

riv - ers,___ poured in - ces - sant from a - bove, and God's

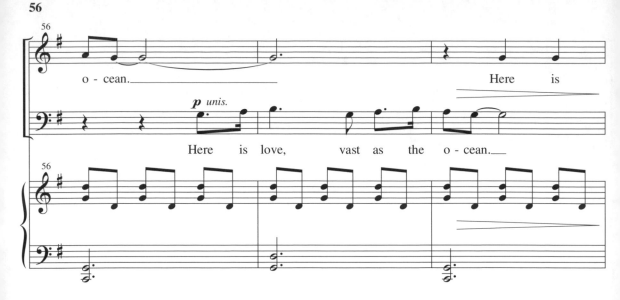

o - cean._____ Here is

p unis.
Here is love, vast as the o - cean.___

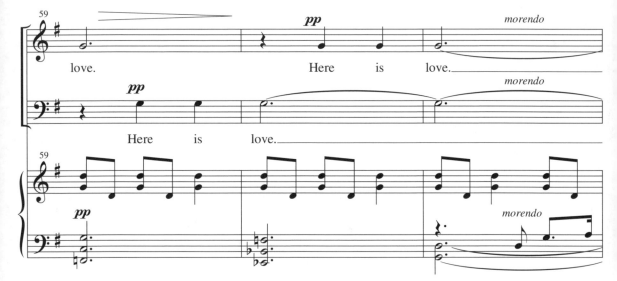

love. *pp* Here is love._____ *morendo*

pp Here is love._____ *morendo*

pp

morendo

rit. *ppp*

ppp

rit.

ppp

CELTIC ALLELUIA

for S.A.T.B. voices, accompanied

Words by
MICHAEL BARRETT

Tunes: **CANDLER**
and **FOREST GREEN**
Arranged by
MICHAEL BARRETT (BMI)
Adapted by
JOSEPH M. MARTIN (BMI)

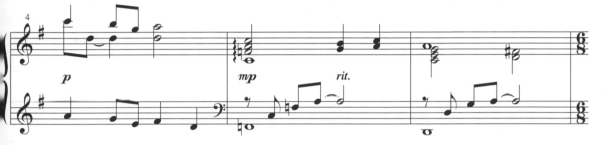

* Tune: FOREST GREEN, Traditional English Melody
** Tune: CANDLER, Traditional Scottish Melody

58

60

Lyrics:
ris - en to-day!

Rise

Rise up! Rise up! Rise up! Rise up! The gar - den is sing - ing. Cre -

up! Rise a - tion is ring - ing with wor - ship and light. Rise

THE CELTIC CHOIR - SATB

death and the grave. Rise up! Rise up!___ New

life now is giv - en, for Je - sus is ris - en, is

ris - en to - day!

* Words: John S. B. Monsell, 1811-1875   THE CELTIC CHOIR - SATB

64

hope and thanks - giv - ing, lift voic - es a - bove. Sing___

al - le - lu - ia! Al - le - lu - ia! Je - sus is Lord o - ver

death and the grave. Rise up! Rise up!___ With

NOT I, BUT CHRIST

for S.A.T.B. voices, accompanied

Words by
ALBERT B. SIMPSON (1843-1919)

Tune: **LONDONDERRY AIR**
Traditional Irish Tune
Arranged by
JOSEPH M. MARTIN (BMI)

70

THE CELTIC CHOIR - SATB

Not I, but Christ, my ev - 'ry need sup -

Oo

74

vi - sion. Glo - ry ex - cel - ling, soon, full soon, I'll

see. Christ, on - ly Christ,_____ my ev - 'ry wish ful -

A CELTIC BLESSING

for S.A.T.B. voices, accompanied

Words:
Traditional Irish Blessing

Music by
PATRICIA THOMPSON
Arranged by
JOSEPH M. MARTIN (BMI)

78